THROUGH THE WIRE

WORDS & LYRICS
KANYE WEST

—

GRAPHIC INTERPRETATIONS
BILL PLYMPTON

ATRIA BOOKS

NEW YORK LONDON TORONTO SYDNEY

ATRIA BOOKS
A DIVISION OF SIMON & SCHUSTER, INC.
1230 AVENUE OF THE AMERICAS
NEW YORK, NY 10020

First Atria Books hardcover edition November 2009

ATRIA BOOKS AND COLOPHON ARE TRADEMARKS OF SIMON & SCHUSTER, INC.

For information about special discounts for bulk purchases,
please contact Simon & Schuster Special Sales at
1-866-506-1949 or business@simonandschuster.com.

The Simon & Schuster Speakers Bureau can bring authors to your live event.
For more information or to book an event, contact the Simon & Schuster Speakers
Bureau at 1-866-248-3049 or visit our website at www.simonspeakers.com

Creative Direction by Kanye West.
Art Direction and Design by Willo Peron and Thomas Mastorakos for Pastelle.

MANUFACTURED IN THE UNITED STATES OF AMERICA

10 9 8 7 6 5 4 3 2 1

Library of Congress Cataloging-in-Publication data is available.

ISBN 978-1-4165-3775-5
ISBN 978-1-4391-8118-8 (ebook)

Due to space limitations, lyric permissions start on page 77
and should be considered an extention of this copyright page.

TABLE OF CONTENTS

DEDICATED
WITH MUCH LOVE TO MY MOTHER,
DR. DONDA WEST

THROUGH THE WIRE

"ALL THEY HEARD WAS THAT I WAS IN AN ACCIDENT LIKE GEICO
THEY THOUGHT I WAS BURNT UP
LIKE PEPSI DID MICHAEL..."

THROUGH THE WIRE

On october 23, 2002, i was in a car accident in los angeles. That's the whole thing. My whole story. I had a big time accident. My jaw was wired shut and that's how I rapped *"through the wire"*—mumbling through the wire on my jaw.

So in this song, I'm recovering from the accident. You know, when your mouth is wired shut you can't eat. But there's this thing from houston, "sippin' on sizzurp," a drink made from cough syrup. But here I use it with pancakes, like maple syrup.

At the time of the accident, I'd already done "h to the izzo" for jay-z. That was my claim to fame.

Emmett till was a black teenager who was murdered in mississippi in 1955. He was brutally killed by a group of white men who claimed that emmett had whistled at a white woman in a convenience store. Emmett's mother refused a closed casket at her son's funeral because she wanted the world to see what those racist assholes had done to her son. The picture of emmett's beat-up face was printed in newspapers around the world.

I'd actually been in a bad car accident before this one, when I was going to pick up my girl from school and I hit black ice and the truck flipped over. That's why I had two lifelines, like on the game show *who wants to be a millionaire?*

Just a few weeks before the accident, I got the deal with roc-a-fella. My girl at the time was in a sorority, delta sigma theta. Their hand sign looks exactly like a roc-a-fella sign.

I was in cedar sinai in l.a., which is the hospital where biggie died, which is also where tupac died.

Michael jackson's hair caught on fire when he was filming a pepsi commercial in the '80s.

LYRICS

Yo G they can't stop me from rapping can they?

Can they, huh?

Through the fire, to the limit, to the wall

For a chance to be with you, I'd gladly risk it all

Through the fire, through whatever come what may

For a chance at loving you, I'd take it all away

Right down through the wire, even through the fire

I spit it through the wire man

Too much stuff on my heart right now man

I'll gladly risk it all right now

It's a life-or-death situation man

Y'all don't really understand how I feel right now man

It's your boy kanye to the . . .

Chi-town what's going on man

I drink a boost for breakfast, and ensure for dizzert

Somebody ordered pancakes i just sip the sizzurp

That right there could drive a sane man bizzerk

Not to worry y'all, mr. H 2 the izzo's back to wizzerk

How do you console my mom or give her light support

When you telling her your son's on life support

And just imagine how my girl feel

On the plane scared as hell that her guy look like
      emmett till

She was with me before the deal, she been trying to be mine

She a delta so she been throwing them dynasty signs

No use me tryin' to be lyin'

I been trying to signed

Trying to be a millionaire

How i use two lifelines

In the same hospital where biggie smalls died

The doctor said i had blood clots

But i ain't jamaican man

Story on mtv and i ain't trying to make the band

I swear this right here is history in the making man

I really apologize how i sound right now man

If it's unclear at all, man

They got my mouth wired shut for like i don't know
      The doctor said for like six weeks

You know we had reconstru . . .

I had reconstructive surgery on my jaw

Looked in the mirror half my jaw was in the back of my mouth
      man

I couldn't believe it

But i'm still here for y'all right now yo

This is what i gotta say yo

Yeah, turn me up yeah

What if somebody from the chi was ill got a deal on the
      hottest rap label around

BUT HE WASN'T TALKING 'BOUT COKE AND BIRDS IT WAS MORE LIKE
    SPOKEN WORD

EXCEPT HE REALLY PUTTING IT DOWN

AND HE EXPLAINED THE STORY ABOUT HOW BLACKS CAME FROM GLORY

AND WHAT WE NEED TO DO IN THE GAME

GOOD DUDE, BAD NIGHT, RIGHT PLACE, WRONG TIME

IN THE BLINK OF AN EYE HIS WHOLE LIFE CHANGED

IF YOU COULD FEEL HOW MY FACE FELT YOU WOULD KNOW HOW MASE
    FELT

THANK GOD I AIN'T TOO COOL FOR THE SAFE BELT

I SWEAR TO GOD DRIVE TWO ON THE SUE

I GOT LAWYER FOR THE CASE TO KEEP WHAT'S IN MY SAFE SAFE

MY DAWGS COULDN'T TELL IF I

I LOOK TOM CRUISE IN VANILLA SKY, IT WAS TELEVISED

ALL THEY HEARD WAS THAT I WAS IN AN ACCIDENT LIKE GEICO

THEY THOUGHT I WAS BURNT UP LIKE PEPSI DID MICHAEL

I MUST GOTTA ANGEL

CAUSE LOOK HOW DEATH MISSED HIS ASS

UNBREAKABLE, WOULD YOU THOUGHT THEY CALLED ME MR. GLASS

LOOK BACK ON MY LIFE LIKE THE GHOST OF CHRISTMAS PAST

TOYS R US WHERE I USED TO SPEND THAT CHRISTMAS CASH

AND I STILL WON'T GROW UP, I'M A GROWN-ASS KID

SWEAR I SHOULD BE LOCKED UP FOR STUPID SHIT THAT I DID

BUT I'M A CHAMPION, SO I TURNED TRAGEDY TO TRIUMPH

MAKE MUSIC THAT'S FIRE, SPIT MY SOUL THROUGH THE WIRE

KNOW WHAT I'M SAYING

WHEN THE DOCTOR TOLD ME I HAD A UM . . . I WAS GOIN' TO HAVE A
    PLATE ON MY CHIN

I SAID DAWG DON'T YOU REALIZE I'LL NEVER MAKE IT ON THE
    PLANE NOW

IT'S BAD ENOUGH I GOT ALL THIS JEWELRY ON

CAN'T BE SERIOUS MAN

SCHOOL SPIRIT

"DO THE SCHOOL STEP, DO WHAT YOU DO, BUT I NEVER PLEDGED THIS SONG IS LIKE MACY'S COMING OUT WITH A COMMERCIAL SAYING GO ON, SPEND YOUR MONEY, GO ON SPEND YOUR MONEY."

SCHOOL SPIRIT

You go to school, you pledge and believe everything they tell you. You go ahead and get your degree and your house in the suburbs and corporate job and 2.5 kids and act like you're going to be happy. Ain't for me.

The title "school spirit" is sarcastic, because there's a lack thereof on this entire album. The cover of *college dropout* has a mascot with its head down.

Do the school step, do what you do, but i never pledged. This song is like macy's coming out with a commercial saying, "go on spend your money, go on spend your money."

LYRICS

School spirit motherfuckers

Alpha, step. Omega, step

Kappa, step. Sigma, step

Gangstas walk, pimps gon' talk

Oooh hecky naw that boy is raw

Aka, step. Delta, step

S g rho, step. Zeta, step

Gangstas walk, pimps gon' talk

Oooh hecky naw that boy is raw

I'ma get on this tv, momma

I'ma, i'ma break shit down

I'ma make sure these light-skinned niggaz

Never ever never come back in style

Told 'em i finished school, and i started my own business

They say, "oh you graduated?"

No, i decided i was finished

Chasin' y'all dreams and what you've got planned

Now i spit it so hot you got tanned

Back to school and i hate it there, i hate it there

Everything i want i gotta wait a year, i wait a year

This nigga graduated at the top of my class

I went to cheesecake, he was a motherfucking waiter there

I got a jones like norah for your soror'

Bring more of them girls i've seen in the aurora

Tammy, becky, and laura, or'a shirley

I'm tryin' to hit it early, like i'm in a hurry

See, that's how dude became the young pootie tang tippy tow

Rocafella chain, yeah that's my rapper style

Rosary piece, yeah that's my catholic style

Red and white one's, yeah that's my kappa style

And i ain't even pledge

Crack my head on the steering wheel and i ain't
    even dead

If i could go through all that and still be breathing

Bitch bend over, i'm here for a reason

"*I WISH I COULD BUY ME A...*

SPACE

E SHIP

...AND FLY PAST THE SKY
I'VE BEEN WORKING THIS GRAVEYARD SHIFT
AND I AIN'T MADE SHIT
I WISH I COULD BUY ME A SPACESHIP
AND FLY PAST THE SKY
MAN, I'M TALKING WAY PAST THE SKY..."

SPACESHIP

At the same time I was working at the Gap, I was working at night in my basement making beats.

I'd had hit records at this point, but I was still working at the Gap, and there was no way I could afford a Maybach. I was still waiting for a chance to take off.

I'm a producer, so I had a lot of old vinyl in my apartment. I was working really hard making beats, investing so much into my career.

This song is all about me working at the Gap. I worked there a few months before they fired me.

LYRICS

I've been workin' this graveshift and I ain't made shit

I wish i could buy me a spaceship and fly past the sky

I've been workin' this graveshift and i ain't made shit

I wish i could buy me a spaceship and fly past the sky

Man, man, man

If my manager insults me again i will be assaulting him

After i fuck the manager up then i'm gonna shorten the register up

Let's go back, back to the gap

Look at my check, wasn't no scratch

So if i stole, wasn't my fault

Yeah i stole, never got caught

They take me to the back and pat me

Askin' me about some khakis

But let some black people walk in

I bet they show off their token blackie

Oh now they love kanye, let's put him all in the front of the store

Saw him on break next to the "no smoking" sign with a blunt and a marl'

Takin' my hits, writin' my hits

Writin' my rhymes, playin' my mind

This fuckin' job can't help him

So i quit, y'all welcome

Y'all don't know my struggle

Y'all can't match my hustle

You can't catch my hustle

You can't fathom my love dude

Lock yourself in a room doin' five beats a day for three summers

That's a different world like cree summers

I deserve to do these numbers

The kid that made that deserves that maybach

So many records in my basement

I'm just waitin' on my spaceship, blow

I've been workin' this graveshift and i ain't made shit

I wish i could buy me a spaceship and fly past the sky

I've been workin' this graveshift and i ain't made shit

I wish i could buy me a spaceship and fly past the sky

Man, i'm talkin' way past the sky

Let's go, yeah

And i didn't even try to work a job

Represent the mob

At the same time thirsty on the grind

Chi state of mind

Lost my momma, lost my mind

My life, my love, that's not mine

Why you ain't signed?

Wasn't my time

Leave me alone, work for y'all

Half of it's yours, half of it's mine

Only one to ball

Never one to fall

Gotta get mine

Gotta take mine

Got a tec nine

Reach my prime

Gotta make these haters respect mine

In the mall 'til 12 when my schedule wore headset nine

Puttin' those pants on shelves

Waitin' patiently i ask myself

Where i wanna go, where i wanna be

Life is much more than runnin' in the streets

Holla at 'ye, hit me with the beat

Put me on my feet

Sound so sweet

Yes i'm the same ol' g, same goatee

Stayin' low key, nope

Holler at god, "man why'd you had to take my folks?"

Hope to see freddy g, yusef g

Love my g, rolly g

Police watch me smoke my weed and count my g's

Got a lot of people countin' on me

And i'm just tryin' to find my peace

Should of finished school like my niece

Then i wouldn't finally wouldn't use my piece

Aw man, this pressure

I've been workin' this graveshift and i ain't made shit

I wish i could buy me a spaceship and fly past the sky

I've been workin' this graveshift and i ain't made shit

I wish i could buy me a spaceship and fly past the sky

ALL FALLS DOWN

"OH WHEN IT ALL, IT ALL FALLS DOWN
I'M TELLING YOU ALL WHEN IT FALLS DOWN
MAN I PROMISE, I'M SO SELF-CONSCIOUS
THAT'S WHY YOU ALWAYS SEE ME
WITH AT LEAST ONE OF MY WATCHES."

ALL FALLS DOWN

She wanted all these things that America says you're supposed to have.
But when you can't get these things, instead you embody them, take
them in a different direction. Like wearing a lot of polos because you
can't actually afford a yacht, but you still want a piece of that life.

I mispronounced "versace" here like in the movie *showgirls* when nomi
says "thanks. It's a ver-sayce."

Now that we got money, we're trying to buy the forty acres that
black people were promised after the civil war but never got. Dave
chappelle made this joke about reparations, that if black people did
get reparations, they'd go out and buy cadillacs and kfc.

It's a nouveau riche thing. Like, even if you do make money, it doesn't
really count unless it's old-school money. Like paris hilton telling
lindsay lohan, "you're broke."

I was actually thinking of oj. He's not really free, he's just out of
jail.

Bill maher tried to say, "i'm a white man, and i'm not getting paid off
anything." I'm talking about "the white man," the imaginary old white
guy in a suit behind a desk.

LYRICS

Man I promise, she's so self-conscious

She has no idea what she's doing in college

That major that she majored in don't make no money

But she won't drop out, her parents will look at
her funny

Now, tell me that ain't insecure

The concept of school seems so secure

Sophomore three years ain't picked a career

She like fuck it, I'll just stay down here and do hair

'Cause that's enough money to buy her a few pairs
of new airs

'Cause her baby daddy don't really care

She's so precious with peer pressure

Couldn't afford a car so she named her daughter alexis

She had hair so long that it looked like weave

Then she cut it all off now she look like eve

And she be dealing with some issues that you
can't believe

Single black female addicted to retail, and well

Oh when it all, it all falls down

I'm telling you all when it all falls down

Man I promise, I'm so self-conscious

That's why you always see me with at least one of
my watches

Rollies and pasha's done drove me crazy

I can't even pronounce nothing, pass that versace!

Then I spent 400 bucks on this

Just to be like nigga, you ain't up on this!

And I can't even go to the grocery store

Without some ones that's clean and a shirt with a team

It seems we living the american dream

But the people highest up got the lowest self-esteem

The prettiest people do the ugliest things

For the road to riches and diamond rings

We shine because they hate us, floss cause they degrade us

We trying to buy back our 40 acres

And for that paper, look how low we a'stoop

Even if you in a benz, you still a nigga in a coupe

I say fuck the police, that's how i treat 'em

We buy our way out of jail, but we can't buy freedom

We'll buy a lot of clothes when we don't really need 'em

Things we buy to cover up what's inside

'Cause they make us hate ourself and love they wealth

That's why shorties hollering, "where the ballas at?"

Drug dealer buy jordans, crackhead buy crack

And a white man get paid off of all of that

But i ain't even goin' act holier than thou

'Cause fuck it, i went to jacob with 25 thou

Before i had a house and i'd do it again

'Cause i wanna be on 106 and park pushing a benz

I WANNA ACT BALLERIFIC LIKE IT'S ALL TERRIFIC

I GOT A COUPLE PAST DUE BILLS, I WON'T GET SPECIFIC

I GOT A PROBLEM WITH SPENDING BEFORE I GET IT

WE ALL SELF-CONSCIOUS I'M JUST THE FIRST TO ADMIT IT

TOUCH THE SKY

"THIS SONG IS REALLY A LETTER TO MY GIRL WHO WAS WITH ME BACK WHEN WE WERE SPLITTING THE BUFFET AT KFC AND WHO SUPPORTED ME IN CHASING MY DREAM. I WANTED TO TELL HER THAT SHE'D FIND HAPPINESS EVEN THOUGH I WAS'NT THE ONE WHO COULD GIVE IT TO HER, AND EVEN THOUGH I CAUSED HER PAIN."

TOUCH THE SKY

PICTURE THIS: ME AND MY MOTHER, PACKING UP EVERYTHING IN MY APARTMENT IN CHICAGO, AND MOVING IT ALL TO AN APARTMENT I'VE NEVER SEEN IN NEWARK, NEW JERSEY. I WANTED TO GO TO NEW YORK CITY, 'CAUSE THAT'S THE MECCA, AND SHE HELPED ME GET THERE. WE PACKED, LOADED UP ALL THAT EQUIPMENT, AND DROVE ACROSS THE COUNTRY. THEN WE WENT TO IKEA AND BOUGHT A BED THAT I HAD TO PUT TOGETHER MYSELF.

I LITERALLY COULDN'T TALK TO THE PESSIMISTS, BECAUSE I REALLY DIDN'T HAVE A PHONE IN MY APARTMENT.

I DIDN'T WANT TO BE THAT GUY ON LINE AT THE CLUB ANY MORE, SO I WENT TO JACOB THE JEWELER SO THAT I COULD WEAR A CHAIN AND WALK RIGHT INTO THE CLUB AND SHINE.

I RHYME "I AM" WITH "TIME." WE PLAY A RHYMING GAME WHERE WE SAY A WORD LIKE "PAT," THEN THE NEXT PERSON SAYS A WORD THAT RHYMES, LIKE "THAT." IT CAN'T BE TWO SYLLABLES. YOU CAN'T REPEAT. IT'S ALL ABOUT SOUND. YOU CAN'T REPEAT "NOT" WITH "KNOT." SOME PEOPLE TRY TO RHYME "THOUGHT" WITH "THAT." UNLESS YOU'RE FROM BOSTON, YOU CAN'T DO THAT. THE GAME'S A GOOD BASIS OF PEOPLE'S CONCEPTS IN LIFE. SOME PEOPLE TRY TO CHEAT AND OTHER PEOPLE DON'T. THE PERSON WHO WINS IS THE ONE WITH THE BEST VOCABULARY.

I QUESTION THAT SOMETIMES. IT'S LIKE, MAYBE THIS IS HEAVEN. FOR ALL I KNOW, THIS IS THE AFTERLIFE. I MOVE LIKE I'M IN A DREAM WORLD. MOST PEOPLE MOVE WITH BOUNDARIES. BUT IF YOU'RE IN A DREAM YOU DON'T HAVE THOSE BOUNDARIES. I SPEAK AND I TALK LIKE THERE AREN'T BOUNDARIES HOLDING ME BACK. HOW ABOUT I'M GOING TO DO WHAT I FEEL.

THERE'S ACTUALLY A DOUBLE MEANING HERE. BAD BOY HAD THIS GROUP THE LOX. THEY WERE REALLY HOT, BUT BAD BOY DIDN'T DO WELL WITH THEM. AND THE STREET TEAM IS THE PROMOTION. THE DOOR WAS REALLY LOCKED FOR ME AND I WAS TRYING TO GET INTO THE BUSINESS.

I bought some Gucci loafers, even though I could barely afford them. You can only get so much cash at an ATM at one time, so I had to use the ATM twice so I could get enough cash for the loafers. They were $425 and I knew I was going to buy them that day. My girl was going to bust me out in the store in front of people by saying, "Well, if you can't afford them, maybe we shouldn't be . . ." and I felt like, what are you trying to do, steal my swagger? But still, the people who work in those stores know the difference. They can recognize people that have money. When people have money, they have a credit card and they can hand it over to buy a lot of different things. When someone comes in and pays for $425 loafers with exactly $425 in cash, they know what's up.

My girl at the time went to school in Missouri, outside of St. Louis. We would go to this mall about forty miles from her school and we hardly had enough money for gas to get there. She'd go to the KFC buffet and I'd sit with her and sneak food off her plate.

It was really tough, dealing with my girl during this time. I hopped on that plane and chased my dream, but at the same time I knew that if I left I'd have to lose my girl. To pursue my dream I had to leave her behind, even though she was the person who supported me and told me to chase that dream.

TOUCH THE SKY | **Lyrics**

LYRICS

I gotta testify, come up in the spot looking extra fly

For the day i die, i'ma touch the sky

Gotta testify, come up in the spot looking extra fly

For the day i die, i'ma touch the sky

Back when they thought pink polos would hurt
the roc,

Before cam got the shit to pop, the doors was closed

I felt like bad boy's street team, i couldn't work
the lox.

Now let's go.

Take 'em back to the plan . . .

Me and my momma hopped in the u-haul van.

Any pessimists i ain't talked to them,

Plus, i ain't have no phone in my apartment.

Let's take 'em back to the club.

Least about an hour i would stand on line,

I just wanted to dance.

I went to jacob an hour after i got my advance.

I just wanted to shine.

Jay's favorite line: "dog, in due time"

Now he look at me, like "damn, dog, you where i am"

A hip-hop legend.

I think i died in an accident, 'cause this must be heaven.

Back when gucci was the shit to rock,

Back when slick rick got the shit to pop,

I'd do anything to say "i got it."

Damn, them new loafers hurt my pocket.

Before anybody wanted k-west beats,

Me and my girl split the buffet at kfc.

Dog, i was having nervous breakdowns,

Like "damn, these niggas that much better than me?"

Baby, i'm going on an airplane,

And i don't know if i'll be back again

Sure enough, i sent the plane tickets

But when she came to kick it, things became different.

Any girl i cheated on, sheets i skeeted on.

I couldn't keep it home, i thought i needed a nia long.

I'm trying to write my wrongs,

But it's funny these same wrongs helped me write
this song.

Now . . .

I gotta testify, come up in the spot looking extra fly

For the day you die, you gonna touch the sky

(You gonna touch the sky babygirl!)

Testify, come up in the spot

Looking extra fly

For the day you die, you gonna touch the sky

THE NEW WORKOUT PLAN

"THAT'S RIGHT PUT IN WORK, MOVE YOUR ASS, GO BERSERK, EAT YOUR SALAD, NO DESSERT GET THAN MAN YOU DESERVE IT'S KANYE'S WORKOUT PLAN"

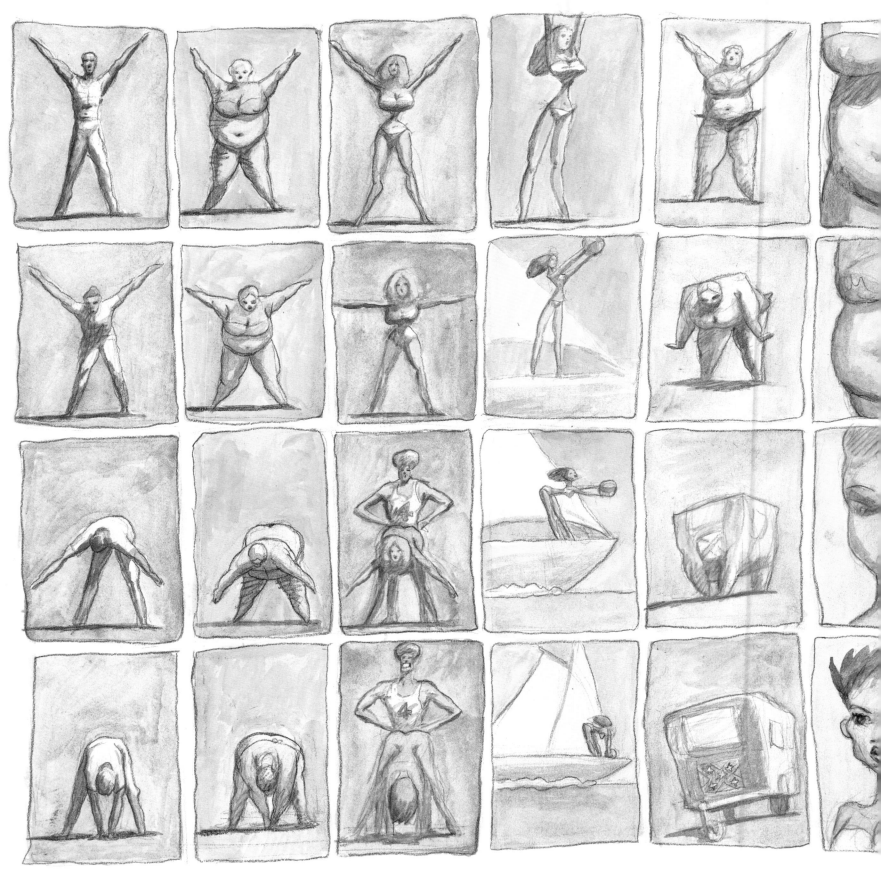

THE NEW WORKOUT PLAN

LYRICS

Now you just popped in the Kanye West

Get right for the summer workout tape

And ladies if you follow these instructions exactly

You might be able to pull you a rapper, a NBA player

Man, at least a dude wit' a car

So first of all we gon' work on the stomach

Nobody wants a little tight ass!

1 And 2 and 3 and 4 and get them sit-ups right and

Tuck your tummy tight and do your crunches like this

Give head, stop breathe, get up, check your weave

Don't drop the blunt and disrespect the weed

Pick up your son and don't disrespect your seed

It's a party tonight and ooh she's so excited

Tell me who's invited: you, your friends, and my dick

What's scary to me, henny make girls look like Halle Berry to
     me

So excuse me miss, i forgot your name

Thank you, god bless you, good night i came . . .

I came . . .

I came . . .

It's been a week without me

And she feel weak without me

She want to talk it out but

Ain't nothin' to talk about

Anless she talkin' 'bout freakin' out

And maybe we can work it out

Work it out

Work it out

Work it out

Work it out nooowww

Maybe we can work it out

Oh girl your silhouette make me wanna light a cigarette

My name kanye from the jigga set twista said get it wet

Ooh girl your breath is harsh

Cover your mouth up like you got sars

Off them tracks, yea, i bought them cars

Still kill a nigga on 16 bars

We ain't sweatin' to the oldies we jukin' to a cold beat

Maybe one day, girl, we can bone

So you can brag to all your homies now

But i still mess with a big girl if you ain't fit girl i still
     hit girl

1 And you brought 2 friends ok 3 more now hop in the benz

4 Door do you know the difference between a 5, 6, 7, 8

All them mocha lattes you gotta do pilates

You gotta pop this tape in before you start back dating

Hustlers, gangstas, all us ballas

Hi my name is Jill, i just want to say thanks to

Kanye's workout plan, i was able to pull a NBA player

And like now i shop every day on rodeo drive

I JUST WANT TO SAY, THANK YOU KANYE! WOOOO! WOOOO! WOOOO!
WOOOO! WOOOO! WOOOO!

MY NAME IS LASANDRA, AND I JUST WANT TO SAY SINCE LISTENIN' TO
KANYE'S WORKOUT TAPE

I WAS ABLE TO GET MY PHONE BILL PAID, I GOT SOUNDS AND 13'S

PUT ON MY CAVALIER AND I WAS ABLE TO GET A FREE TRIP TO CANCUN

AND WHAT'S MOST IMPORTANTLY IS THAT I AIN'T GOTTA FUCK WIT' RAY-
RAY'S BROKE ASS NO MO'

(WORK IT OUT, JUKE IT OUT, PUMP IT OUT, CHI-TOWN OUT,
LET'S GO OUT)

MY NAME IS ELLA-MAY FROM MOBILE, ALABAMA

AND I JUST WANT TO SAY SINCE LISTENIN' TO KANYE'S
WORKOUT TAPE

I BEEN ABLE TO DATE OUTSIDE THE FAMILY, I GOT A DOUBLE WIDE

AND I RODE A PLANE, RODE A PLANE, RODE A PLANE, RODE A PLANE,
RODE A PLANE

THANKS TO KANYE'S WORKOUT PLAN

I'M THE ENVY OF ALL MY FRIENDS

SEE I PULLED ME A BALLA MAN (YEAH)

AND I DON'T GOTTA WORK AT THE MALL AGAIN

(LEMME BREAK Y'ALL OFF A PIECE OF)

MY FAVORITE WORK OUT PLAN (OH! OH! OH!)

I WANNA SEE YOU WORK OUT (YEAH YEAH YEAH YEAH, YEAH YEAH YEAH
YEAH)

(IT'S LIKE THAT OLD MICHAEL JACKSON SHIT)

THAT'S RIGHT PUT IN WORK, MOVE YOUR ASS, GO BERSERK

EAT YOUR SALAD, NO DESSERT

GET THAT MAN YOU DESERVE

IT'S KANYE'S WORKOUT PLAN

I SAID IT'S KANYE'S WORKOUT PLAN (LADIES AND GENTLEMEN)

IT'S KANYE'S WORKOUT PLAN (ALLOW MYSELF TO INTRODUCE MYSELF)

HIS WOOOORRRRKKOOUUT PLAN (THIS TIME AROUND I WANT Y'ALL TO
CLAP LIKE THIS)

THAT'S RIGHT PUT IN WORK

MOVE YOUR ASS, GO BERSERK

EAT YOUR SALAD, NO DESSERT

GET THAT MAN YOU DESERVE (AND STOP!)

IT'S KANYE'S WORKOUT PLAN (OK BRING)

I SAID IT'S KANYE'S WORKOUT PLAN (I KNOW Y'ALL AIN'T TIRED)

IT'S KANYE'S WORKOUT PLAN (BUT I HOPE NOT, 'CUZ ON THIS ONE
I NEED Y'ALL)

HIS WOOOORRRRKKOOUUT PLAN (TO GIVE ME A SOUL CLAP OK? DOUBLE
TIME)

THAT'S RIGHT PUT IN WORK (WOO!)

MOVE YOUR ASS, GO BEZZERK

EAT YOUR SALAD, NO DESSERT

GET THAT MAN YOU DESERVE

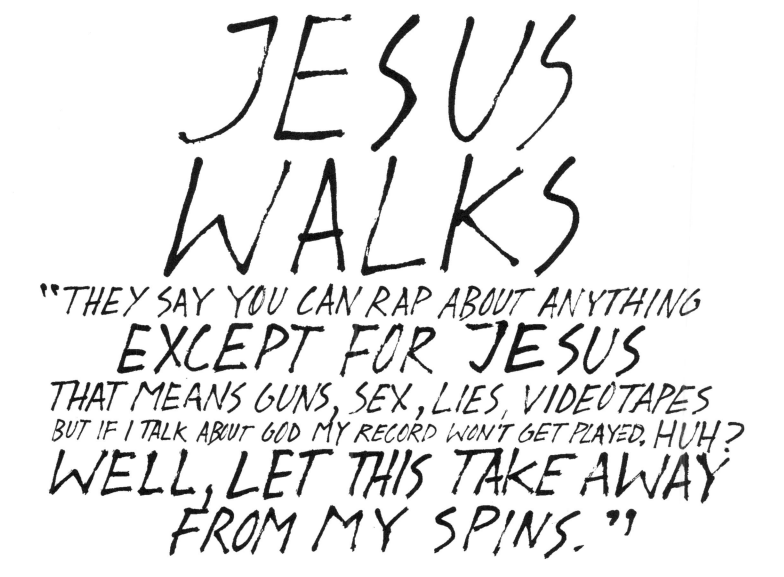

JESUS WALKS

"THEY SAY YOU CAN RAP ABOUT ANYTHING EXCEPT FOR JESUS THAT MEANS GUNS, SEX, LIES, VIDEOTAPES BUT IF I TALK ABOUT GOD MY RECORD WON'T GET PLAYED, HUH? WELL, LET THIS TAKE AWAY FROM MY SPINS."

JESUS WALKS

THIS SONG IS WRITTEN FROM THE PERSPECTIVE OF A DRUG DEALER. "GONE TO NOVEMBER" WAS A SONG THAT WYCLEF MADE REPRESENTING A DRUG DEALER GOING DOWN SOUTH.

"HUH? YOU EAT PIECES OF SHIT?" THAT'S AN ADAM SANDLER JOKE, FROM *HAPPY GILMORE*.

I WOULD GO TO STRIP CLUBS AND STRIPPERS WOULD SAY, "HOW YOU GONNA PUT US IN THERE WITH THE MURDERERS AND DRUG DEALERS?"

"SEE THEE MORE CLEARLY," I GOT THAT FROM *MEET THE PARENTS*. IT'S WEIRD HOW THE REALLY SERIOUS SONGS HAVE POP REFERENCES.

THEY TRIED TO GET ME TO CHANGE "KATHIE LEE" TO "KELLY" WHEN I PERFORMED THIS SONG ON *THE TODAY SHOW*.

I'M CALLING THEM OUT. THIS LINE WAS SOME REVERSE PSYCHOLOGY TO GET RADIO STATIONS TO PLAY THE SONG. YOU CAN RAP OUT ANYTHING EXCEPT JESUS, RIGHT?

LYRICS

Yo, we at war

We at war with terrorism, racism, and most of all we at war
with ourselves

(Jesus walks)

God show me the way because the devil trying to break me
down

(Jesus walks with me) with me, with me, with me

You know what the midwest is?

Young & restless

Where restless niggas might snatch your necklace

And next these niggas might jack your lexus

Somebody tell these niggas who kanye west is

I walk through the valley of the chi where death is

Top floor the view alone will leave you breathless uhhhh!

Try to catch it uhhhh! It's kinda hard hard

Getting choked by the detectives yeah yeah now check
the method

They be asking us questions, harass and arrest us

Saying, "we eat pieces of shit like you for breakfast"

Huh? Y'all eat pieces of shit? What's the basis?

We ain't going nowhere but got suits and cases

A trunk full of coke rental car from avis

My momma used to say only jesus can save us

Well momma i know i act a fool

But i'll be gone 'til november i got packs to move i hope

(Jesus walks)

God show me the way because the devil trying to break
me down

(Jesus walks with me)

The only thing that that i pray is that my feet don't fail
me now

(Jesus walks)

And i don't think there is nothing i can do now to right
my wrongs

(Jesus walks with me)

I want to talk to god but i'm afraid because we ain't spoke
in so long

To the hustlas, killers, murderers, drug dealers, even
the strippers

(Jesus walks with them)

To the victims of welfare for we living in hell here hell yeah

(Jesus walks with them)

Now hear ye hear ye want to see thee more clearly

I know he hear me when my feet get weary

'Cuz we're the almost nearly extinct

We rappers are role models we rap we don't think

I ain't here to argue about his facial features

Or here to convert atheists into believers

I'm just trying to say the way school need teachers

The way kathie lee needed regis that's the way y'all
need jesus

So here go my single dog radio needs this

They say you can rap about anything except for Jesus

That means guns, sex, lies, videotapes

But if i talk about god my record won't get played huh?

Well let this take away from my spins

Which will probably take away from my ends

Then i hope this take away from my sins

And bring the day that i'm dreaming about

Next time i'm in the club everybody screaming out

(Jesus walks)

God show me the way because the devil trying to break me down

(Jesus walks)

The only thing that that i pray is that my feet don't fail me now

(Jesus walks)

And i don't think there's nothing i can do now to right my wrongs

(Jesus walks with me)

The only thing that i pray is that my feet don't fail Me now

HPION

"...CAUSE EVERY SUMMER HE'D GET SOME BRAND NEW HAIRBRAIN SCHEME AND I DUNNO WHAT HE DID FOR DOUGH BUT HE WOULD SEND ME BACK TO SCHOOL WITH A NEW WARDROBE..."

CHAMPION

My dad was always coming up with new ways to get rich quick, including one scheme that involved selling vacuum cleaners, kind of like Will Smith's character in Pursuit of Happyness.

These two lines could be a whole song, there's so much meaning: *"When it feel like living's harder than dying / for me, giving up's way harder than trying."* To have something and quit on it and to think, "Damn, I didn't even try," that's very hard for me. I'd rather try hard and fail. The real failure's never trying.

Lauryn Hill has a famous song about her son Zion with a chorus that goes, "Now the joy of my world is in Zion." She had such a positive message. She's really a genius, a really special person. I wish she were still making music.

Prince used to have his ass hanging out of his clothes, but now he's considered "safe," safe enough for the Super Bowl.

LYRICS

Did you realize . . . that you were a champion in their eyes?

Yes I did

So I packed I up and brought it back to the crib

Just a little somethin' show you how we live

Everybody want it but it ain't that serious

Um hum

That's that shit

So if you goin' do it

Do it just like this

You don't see just how wild the crowd is

You don't see just how fly my style is

I don't see why I need a stylist

When I shop so much I could speak italian

I don't know, I just wanted better for my kids

And I ain't saying we was from the projects

But every time I went a lay-a-way or a deposit

My dad would say when you see clothes, close
   your eyelids

We was sort of like will smith and his son

In the movie, I ain't talkin' 'bout the rich ones

'Cause every summer he'd get some brand new hairbrain scheme

To get rich from

And I dunno what he did for dough

But he would send me back to school with a
   new wardrobe

I think he did

When he packed it up and brought it back to the crib

Just a little something show you how we live

Everything i wanted man it seemed so serious

That's that shit

So if you gonna do it

Do it just like this

When it feel like living's harder than dying

For me, giving up's way harder than trying

Lauryn hill said her heart was in zion

I wish her heart still was in rhyming

Cause who the kids goin' listen to, hug

I guess me if it isn't you

Last week i paid a visit to the institute

They got the dropout keeping kids in the school

I guess i cleaned up my act like prince would do

If not for the pleasure at least for the principle

They got the cd

Then got to see me drop gems, like i dropped out of P.E.

They used to fee invisible

Now they know they invincible

GOLD
DIGGER

"...IF YOU FUCKIN' WITH THIS GIRL,
THEN YOU BETTER BE PAID. NOW I AINT SAYIN'
SHE A GOLD DIGGER
BUT SHE AIN'T MESSIN' WIT' NO BROKE NIGGAZ..."

GOLD DIGGER

LYRICS

She take my money when I'm in need

Yea she's a triflin' friend indeed

Oh she's a gold digga way over town

That digs on me

(She gives me money)

Now I ain't sayin' she a gold digger (when I'm in need)

But she ain't messin' wit' no broke niggaz

(She gives me money)

Now I ain't sayin' she a gold digger (when I'm in need)

But she ain't messin' wit' no broke niggaz

Get down girl gone head get down (I gotta leave)

Get down girl gone head get down (I gotta leave)

Get down girl gone head get down (I gotta leave)

Get down girl gone head

Cutie the bomb

Met her at a beauty salon

With a baby louis vuitton

Under her underarm

She said i can tell you ROC

I can tell by ya charm

Far as girls you got a flock

I can tell by ya charm and ya arm

But i'm lookin for the one

Have you seen her

My psychic told me she have a ass like Serena

Trina, jennifer lopez, four kids

An' i gotta take all they bad ass to show-biz

Ok get ya kids but then they got their friends

I pulled up in the benz, they all got up in

We all went to den and then i had to pay

If you fuckin' with this girl then you betta be payed

You know why

It take too much to touch her

From what i heard she got a baby by busta

My best friend say she use to fuck wit' usher

I don't care what none of y'all say i still love her

(She gives me money)

Now i ain't sayin' she a gold digger (when i'm in need)

But she ain't messin' wit' no broke niggaz

(She gives me money)

Now i ain't sayin' she a gold digger (when i'm in need)

But she ain't messin' wit' no broke niggaz

Get down girl gone head get down (i gotta leave)

Get down girl gone head get down (i gotta leave)

Get down girl gone head get down (i gotta leave)

Get down girl gone head

18 years, 18 years

She got one of yo' kids, got you for 18 years

I know somebody payin' child support for one of his kids

His baby momma's car and crib is bigger than his

You will see him on TV, any given Sunday

Win the super bowl and drive off in a Hyundai

She was s'pose to buy ya shorty Tyco with ya money

She went to the doctor got lypo with ya money

She walkin' around lookin' like Michael with ya money

Should of got that insured, got GEICO for ya money

If you ain't no punk holla "we want prenup"

WE WANT PRENUP! Yeaah

It's something that you need to have

'Cause when she leave yo' ass she gone leave with half

18 years, 18 years

And on her 18th birthday he found out it wasn't his

Now I ain't sayin' she a gold digger

But she ain't messin' wit' no broke niggas

Now I ain't sayin' she a gold digger (when I'm in need)

But she ain't messin' wit' no broke niggas

Get down girl gone head get down

Get down girl gone head get down

Get down girl gone head get down

Get down girl gone head

Now I ain't sayin' you a gold digger you got needs

You don't want ya dude to smoke but he can't buy weed

You got out to eat and he cant pay y'all can't leave

There's dishes in the back, he gotta roll up his sleeves

But why y'all washin' watch him

He gone make it into a benz out of that Datsun

He got that ambition baby look in his eyes

This week he moppin' floorz next week it's the fries

So, stick by his side

I know his dude's ballin' but yea that's nice

And they gone keep callin' and tryin'

But you stay right girl

But when you get on he leave yo ass for a white girl

Get down girl gone head get down

Get down girl gone head get down

Get down girl gone head get down

Get down girl gone head

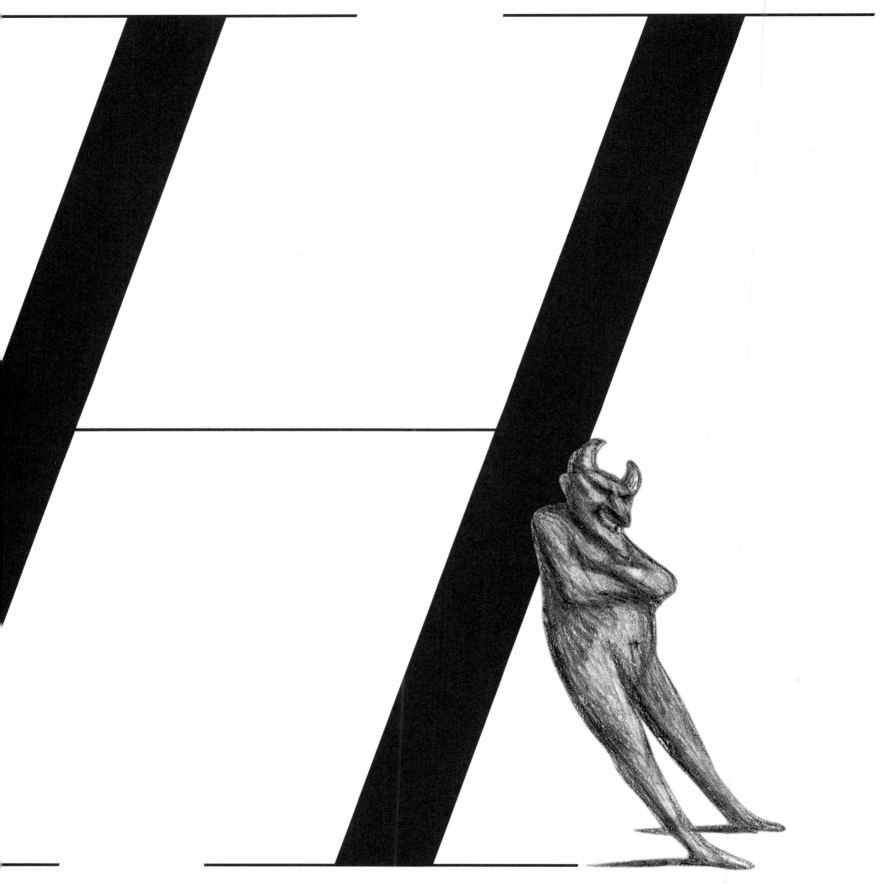

HEARD 'EM SAY

"... AND GRAN KEEP PRAYIN AND KEEP BELIEVIN',
AND JESUS AND ONE DAY THAT YOU SEE HIM,
TILL THEY WALK IN HIS FOOTSTEPS AND TRY TO BE HIM,
THE DEVIL IS ALIVE
I FEEL HIM BREATHIN'..."

HEARD 'EM SAY

LYRICS

And I heard 'em say, nothin' ever promised tomorrow today.

From the chi, like tim it's the hard- a-way,

So this is in the name of love, like robert says

Before you ask me to get a job today, can i at least get a raise on a minimum wage?

And i know the government administered AIDS,

So i guess we just pray like the minister say,

Allah o akbar and throw 'em some hot cars,

Things we see on the screen are not ours,

But these niggas from the hood so these dreams not far,

Where i'm from, the dope boys is the rock stars,

But they can't cop cars without seein' cop cars,

I guess they want us all behind bars.

I know it.

Uh, and i heard 'em say, nothin' ever promised tomorrow today.

(ooooooooo)

And i heard 'em say, nothin' ever promised tomorrow today.

(Nothing's ever promised tomorrow today.)

But we'll find a way

(And nothing lasts forever but be honest babe, it hurts but it may be the only way)

They say people in your life are seasons,

And anything that happen is for a reason,

And niggas guns a-clappin' and keep to squeezin',

And gran keep prayin' and keep believin',

And jesus and one day that ya see him,

Till they walk in his footsteps and try to be him,

The devil is alive i feel him breathin',

Claimin' money is the key so keep on dreamin',

And put them lottery tickets just to tease us,

My aunt pam can't put those cigarettes down,

Now my li'l cousin smokin' those cigarettes now,

His job trying to claim that he too niggerish now,

Is it 'cuz his skin blacker than licorice now?

I can't figure it out . . .

I'm stickin around . . .

('Cuz every worthless word we get more far away, and nothing's ever promised tomorrow today,

And nothing lasts forever but be honest babe, it hurts but it may be the only way)

HEY MAMA

"...THIS IS THE STORY
A MOTHER AND FATHER DIVORCING,
OF AN ONGOING THEME
OF US PACKING UP THE CAR WITH BOXES AND MOVING AWAY."

HEY MAMA

This is the story of a mother and son. It's the story of my mother and father divorcing, of an on-going theme of us packing up the car with boxes and moving away.

I rhyme "doctorate" with "chocolate." Most rappers would never use the word "doctorate." It's an uncool word.

LYRICS

(Hey mama), I wanna scream so loud for you, 'cuz I'm so proud of you

Let me tell you what I'm about to do, (hey mama)

I know I act a fool but, I promise you I'm goin' back to school

I appreciate what you allowed for me

I just want you to be proud of me (hey mama)

I wanna tell the whole world about a friend of mine

This little light of mine and I'm finna let it shine

I'm finna take y'all back to them better times

I'm finna talk about my mama if y'all don't mind

I was three years old, when you and I moved to the Chi

Late December, harsh winter gave me a cold

You fixed me up something that was good for my soul

Famous homemade chicken soup, can I have another bowl?

You work late nights just to keep on the lights

Mommy got me training wheels so I could keep on my bike

And you would give anything in this world

Michael Jackson leather and a glove, but didn't give me a curl

And you never put no man over me

And I love you for that mommy can't you see?

Seven years old, caught you with tears in your eyes

Cuz a nigga cheatin', telling you lies, then I started to cry

As we knelt on the kitchen floor

I said mommy Ima love you till you don't hurt no more

And when I'm older, you aint gotta work no more

And Ima get you that mansion that we couldn't afford

See you're unbreakable, unmistakable

Highly capable, lady that's makin' loot

A livin' legend too, just look at what heaven do

Send us an angel, and I thank you (hey mama)

Forrest gump mama said, life is like a box of chocolates

My mama told me go to school, get your doctorate

Somethin' to fall back on, you could profit with

But still supported me when I did the opposite

Now I feel like it's things I gotta get

Things I gotta do, just to prove to you

You was getting through, can the choir please

Give me a verse of "you are so beautiful to me"

Can't you see, you're like a book of poetry

Maya angelou, nikki giovanni, turn one page and there's my mommy

Come on mommy just dance wit' me, let the whole world see your dancing feet

Now when i say, "hey," y'all say "mama," now everybody answer me (hey mama)

I guess it also depends tho', if my ends low

Second they get up you gon' get that benzo

Tint the windows, ride around the city and let ya friends know (hey mama)

Tell your job you gotta fake 'em out

Since you brought me in this world, let me take you out

To a restaurant, upper echelon

Ima get you a jag, whatever else you want

Just tell me what kind of S-type Donda West like?

Tell me the perfect color so I make it just right

It don't gotta be Mother's Day, or your birthday

For me to just call and say (hey mama)

Forrest Gump mama said, life is like a box of chocolates

My mama told me go to school, get your doctorate

Somethin' to fall back on, you could profit with

But still supported me when I did the opposite

Now I feel like it's things I gotta get

Things I gotta do, just to prove to you

You was getting through, can the choir please

Give me a verse of "you are so beautiful to me"

Can't you see, you're like a book of poetry

Maya Angelou, Nikki Giovanni, turn one page and there's my
    mommy

Come on mommy just dance wit' me, let the whole world see
    your dancing feet

Now when I say, "hey," y'all say "mama," now everybody answer
    me (hey mama)

I guess it also depends tho', if my ends low

Second they get up you gon' get that benzo

Tint the windows, ride around the city and let ya friends know
    (hey mama)

Tell your job you gotta fake 'em out

Since you brought me in this world, let me take you out

To a restaurant, upper echelon

Ima get you a jag, whatever else you want

Just tell me what kind of S-type Donda West like?

Tell me the perfect color so I make it just right

It don't gotta be Mother's Day, or your birthday

For me to just call and say (hey mama)

HOME COMING

"THIS IS A SONG THAT SOUNDS LIKE I'M TALKING ABOUT A GIRL, BUT I'M ACTUALLY TALKING ABOUT CHICAGO THE WHOLE TIME."

HOME COMING

This is a song that sounds like I'm talking about a girl, but I'm actually talking about Chicago the whole time.

Chicago is a really gang-affiliated city, so you have to wear your hat straight when you're there, because if you wear it to one side or the other that means that you're part of a gang.

LYRICS

I met this girl when I was three years old

And what I love most, she had so much soul

She said, "excuse me little homie, I know you don't know me, but

My name is windy, and I like to blow trees."

And from that point I never blow her off

Niggas come from outta town, I like to show her off.

They like to act tough, she like to tell 'em off.

And make them straighten up their hat, 'cause she know they're soft.

And when I grew up she showed me how to go downtown.

And at nighttime my face lit up

So astounding

I told her in my heart where she always be

She never mess with entertainers 'cause they always leave

She said it felt like they walked and drove on me

Knew I was gang-affiliated, got on tv and told on me

I guess that's why last winter she got so cold on me

She said, "Yeah keep making that platinum and gold for me"

But if you really care for her, then you would've never hit the airport

To follow your dreams

Sometimes I still talk to her, but when I talk to her

It always seem that she's talking about me

She said, "You left your kids and they just like you

They want to rap and make soul beats, just like you"

But they just not you, and I just got through, talking 'bout what niggas trying to do

Just not new

Everybody got their gang figured out all wrong

Guess you never know what you got 'til it's gone

Guess that's why i'm here and i can't come back home

And guess when I heard that, when I was back home

Every interview i'm representing you, making you proud

Reach for the stars so if you fall you land on a cloud

Jump in the crowd, spark your lighters, wave them around

If you don't know by now, i'm talking about Chi-town

CREDITS

THROUGH THE WIRE
(D. FOSTER, T. KEANE, C. WEIL)

Warner-Tamerlane Publishing Corp. (BMI)/Dyad Music Ltd./Neropub Music (BMI)/Wixen Music Publishing (BMI)

"Through the Wire" contains a sample from the Chaka Khan recording "Through the Fire." Produced under license from Warner Bros. Records Inc. By arrangement with Warner Strategic Marketing. Written by David Foster, Tom Keane and Cynthia Weil. Published by Warner-Tamerlane Publishing Corp./Dyad Music Ltd./Neropub Music (BMI).

SCHOOL SPIRIT
(K. WEST, A ANKLIN)

Gimme My Publishing, Inc./EMI Blackwood (BMI)/Springtime Music Inc. (BMI)

"School Spirit" contains a sample of the Aretha Franklin recording "Spirit in the Dark." Produced under license from Atlantic Recording Corp. By arrangement with Warner Strategic Marketing. Written by A. Franklin, published by Springtime Music Inc. (BMI).

SPACESHIP
(K. WEST, T. WILLIAMS, L. HARRIS, D. MILLS, M. GAYE, G. GORDY, S. GREENE)

Gimme My Publishing, Inc./EMI Blackwood (BMI)/Tony Williams Pub. Designee/Leonard Harris Pub. Designee/Get Ya Frog On (BMI)/ EMI April Music Inc./Jobete Music Co., Inc. (ASCAP)

"Spaceship" contains a sample of the recording "Distant Lover" performed by Marvin Gaye. Used courtesy of Motown Records, under license from Universal Music Enterprises, a division of UMG Recordings, Inc. Written by M. Gaye, G. Gordy, and S. Greene, published by EMI April Music Inc./ Jobete Music Co., Inc. (ASCAP).

ALL FALLS DOWN
(K. WEST, L. HILL)

Gimme My Publishing, Inc./EMI Blackwood (BMI)/Sony/ATV Tunes, LLC (BMI)

"All Falls Down" contains an interpolation of "Mystery Of Iniquity," Written by Lauryn Hill, published by Sony/ATV Tunes, LLC (BMI).

TOUCH THE SKY
(K. WEST, J. SMITH, W. JACO, C. MAYFIELD)

Please Gimme My Publishing, Inc./EMI Blackwood (BMI)/N.Q.C. Music Publishing (ASCAP) o/b/o F.O.B. Music Publishing (ASCAP)/ Heavy As Heaven Music (BMI)/Warner-Tamerlane Publishing Corp. (BMI)

"Touch The Sky" contains samples from the Curtis Mayfield recording "Move On Up." Produced under license from Atlantic Recording Corp. by arrangement with Warner Strategic Marketing. Written by C. Mayfield, published by Warner-Tamerlane Publishing Corp. (BMI). All rights reserved.

THE NEW WORKOUT PLAN
(K. WEST, J. STEPHENS, B. KANTE, S. RAINEY, M. BEN-ARI)

Gimme My Publishing, Inc./EMI Blackwood (BMI)/Crowded Air Music (ASCAP)/Puzzled Pieces of Mind Music (ASCAP)/Sameka Rainey Pub. Designee/Songs of Universal, Inc./Mirimode Music (BMI)

JESUS WALKS
(K. WEST, C. SMITH, M. BEN-ARI, C. LUNDY)

Gimme My Publishing, Inc./EMI Blackwood (BMI)/Solomon Ink (ASCAP)/Songs of Universal, Inc./Mirimode Music (BMI)/Curtis Lundy Pub. Designee

"Jesus Walks" contains a sample of "Walk With Me" performed by the Arc Choir. Used courtesy of Mapleshade Productions. Arranged by Curtis Lundy. Appears on the CD Walk With Me (Mapleshade 04132).

CHAMPION
(W. BECKER, D. FAGEN)

Universal Music Corp. (ASCAP)

Contains elements of the Steely Dan recording "Kid Charlemagne" used courtesy of Geffen Records under license from Universal Music Enterprises. Written by Walter Becker and Donald Fagen and published by Universal Music Corp. (ASCAP).

GOLD DIGGER
(K. WEST, R. CHARLES, R. RICHARD)

Please Gimme My Publishing, Inc./EMI Blackwood (BMI)/Unichappell Music, Inc. (BMI)/Mijac Music (BMI)

"Gold Digger" contains samples from the Ray Charles recording of "I Got a Woman." Produced under license from Atlantic Recording Corp. by arrangement with Warner Strategic Marketing. Written by R. Charles and R. Richard, Unichappell Music, Inc. (BMI) & Mijac Music (BMI). All rights administered by Unichappell Music, Inc. (BMI). All rights reserved.

HEARD 'EM SAY
"Heard 'Em Say" Featuring Adam Levine Of Maroon 5
(K. WEST, A. LEVINE, M. MASSER, G. GOFFIN)

Please Gimme My Publishing, Inc./EMI Blackwood (BMI)/Careers BMG Music Publishing/February Twenty Second Music (BMI)/Screen Gems-EMI Music Inc. (BMI) and BMG Songs Inc. (ASCAP)

"Heard 'Em Say" contains excerpts from "Someone That I Used to Love" as performed by Natalie Cole. Used courtesy of Capitol Records, under license from EMI Music Marketing. Written by M. Masser and G. Goffin, published by Screen Gems-EMI Music Inc. (BMI) and BMG Songs Inc. (ASCAP)

HEY MAMA
(K. WEST, D. LEACE)

Please Gimme My Publishing, Inc./EMI Blackwood (BMI)/ATL Music (ASCAP)

"Hey Mama" contains samples from the Donal Leace recording "Today Won't Come Again." Produced under license from Atlantic Recording Corp., by arrangement with Warner Strategic Marketing. Written by Donal Leace, used courtesy of ATL Music

HOMECOMING
(K. WEST, C. MARTIN, W. CAMPBELL, A. WILLIAMS)

Please Gimme My Publishing, Inc./EMI Blackwood (BMI)/BMG Songs, Inc. (ASCAP)/Wet Ink Red Music (ASCAP)/ Penafire (BMI)